Contents

Introduction
What is the
Church?

Some people think that the church is a building. There *are* buildings called churches: special places where Christians meet to worship God.

They may have spires or towers, pillars and arches. They may have coloured windows, and the coloured glass may make a picture. Inside you might see carvings and candlesticks, and perhaps a cross ...

Another church building might be quite plain, with bare white walls inside and rows of hard wooden seats ...

Another might be a bright modern room with comfortable chairs arranged in a circle ...

But if the building is empty, the real church isn't there ...

A First Look

THE
CHURCH

Lois Rock

Illustrated by Carolyn Cox

Educational consultant: Margaret Dean

A LION BOOK

Bible passages mentioned in this book:

1   Romans, chapter 8, verses 5 to 15

2   1 Peter, chapter 3, verse 21

3   Matthew, chapter 26, verses 26 to 30, Mark chapter 14, verses 22 to 26, Luke chapter 22, verses 14 to 20; See also 1 Corinthians, chapter 11, verses 23 to 25

4   Hebrews, chapter 10, verse 25

5   Colossians, chapter 3, verse 16

6   1 John, chapter 1, verse 9

7   1 Peter, chapter 1, verse 3

8   Philippians, chapter 4, verse 6

9   Romans, chapter 12, verses 6 to 14

10 Colossians, chapter 3, verse 16

11 Matthew, chapter 28, verse 19

12 Philippians, chapter 2, verse 15

13 Romans, chapter 8, verses 38 to 39

Text by Lois Rock
Copyright © 1994 Lion Publishing
Illustrations copyright © 1994 Carolyn Cox

The author asserts the moral right
to be identified as the author of this work

Published by
Lion Publishing plc
Sandy Lane West, Oxford, England
ISBN 0 7459 2499 9
Albatross Books Pty Ltd
PO Box 320, Sutherland, NSW 2232, Australia
ISBN 0 7324 0737 0

First edition 1994

A catalogue record for this book is available from the British Library

Printed and bound in Singapore

The church is all the people who believe in Jesus Christ. They are called Christians.

There have been people called Christians for nearly 2,000 years, in many parts of the world. They meet in all kinds of church buildings and have different ways of worshipping God.

The special book of their faith, the Bible, explains how people first became Christians, how Christians should live, and what they should do together as a church.

In this book you will find out some of the things the Bible says about the church. It explains—

● what a Christian is

● why Christians meet together

● what they do at their meetings

● how their beliefs change the way they behave

● the message they want to tell other people

1 Let's look at
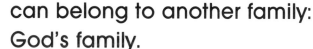
Families

Brothers and sisters
are different from friends.
They have been born into
or made into
a family.
They belong to each other.

Everyone is part of a human family.
The Bible says that people
can belong to another family:
God's family.

It's only human to do wrong things.
That cannot please God
because God is good.
But Jesus came
to help people change,
to put things right
between them and God.
When people believe that,
God makes them his children
and they can call God
Daddy.

From the letter Paul wrote to the
first Christians in Rome

Every Christian belongs
to God's family.
God is their father.
Other Christians are their
brothers and sisters.

The church is the family
of Christians.

2 Let's look at
New beginnings

Some days
everything goes wrong.
If only you could begin the day again.
If only you could be good.

Christians believe
that God helps people start again.

There is a special event
called baptism
when people are washed
with water
to show they are making
a new start
as God's children.

Baptism is not the washing away
of ordinary dirt;
it is the sign of a new beginning
and a promise to live in a way
that pleases God.

From the first letter Peter wrote to new Christians

**When people join God's family,
the church, they are making a
new beginning.**

3 Let's look at
Remembering

Does your family celebrate special events?
Do you have a meal together
and talk about what you are celebrating?
Do you say: 'Do you remember...?'

When they meet as a church,
the Christian family
shares a special meal.

This is how it began.

It was the time of a Jewish celebration called the Passover. Jesus was sharing a meal with his friends. He took a loaf, broke it into pieces and shared it out.

'Eat this now,' he said. 'And every time you share bread together like this, remember I have given my life for you.'

Then he took a cup of wine, and shared it with them. 'Drink this,' he said. 'And when you share wine like this, remember I have given my life for you.'

From the books that Matthew, Mark and Luke wrote about Jesus

The very next day, Jesus was killed. But God brought him to life again. Christians believe that those who follow Jesus start a new life too: a new life as God's friends for ever.

Christians share bread and wine as a church, to remember Jesus — and that he gave his life for them.

4 Let's look at

Being together

It's great when everyone in a family gets together
to talk, to share news, to do things.
You can help each other,
learn from each other,
have fun being together.

The Bible says
that the family of Christians
must meet together too.
Christians cannot help each other
if they never meet.

We, the family of God,
should be concerned about each other.
And we shouldn't forget to meet together—
as some do—
but get together to encourage each other.

From the letter written to a group of Hebrew Christians

Christians meet as a church to
help and encourage each other.

5 Let's look at

Learning together

It's fun to find things out for
yourself.
But it can be easier
to learn new things
from someone who really
knows.
And it's good to find out more
with people who are learning
just like you.

Christians want to find out more about God
and how he wants them to live:
how to show their love for him,
how to show their love for others.

When they meet as a
church, they can learn
together.
Those that are good at
teaching
can help beginners
understand more.
Christians can read the
Bible together
and learn what it means.

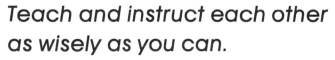

*Teach and instruct each other
as wisely as you can.*

**From the letter Paul wrote to the
first Christians in the city of Colossae**

**Christians learn about God — on
their own and together as a
church.**

6 Let's look at
Saying sorry

When you do something wrong
you often wish you hadn't.
Then you want to say sorry
to those you have hurt.
You want them to forgive you,
so that the wrong thing can be
put right
and then forgotten.

If a group of people
have done wrong things
they may get together to say sorry
so that they can help each other
to do the right thing next time.

Christians are sad
when they do something wrong,
something that is not what God
wants. They know they must say
sorry to God as well as to the
person they have hurt.

They want to tell him how sorry they are that they have done wrong things. They know that God will forgive them and help them to do what is right.

From the first letter John wrote to new Christians

Christians say sorry to God for the wrong things they have done — on their own and together as a church.

7 Let's look at
Thank-yous

When someone gives you a present,
or does something really kind,
you want to say thank you.
It shows the person
how happy you are
and it makes them happy too.

When Christians meet
they say thank you to God:
for the world he has made
and all the good things it provides;
for being a loving father to them,
for helping and guiding them
in all they do.

*Let us always give thanks to God
who has given us new life.*
From the first letter Peter wrote to new Christians

**Christians say thank you to God for
his goodness to them — on their
own and together as a church.**

8 Let's look at

Asking

Dare you ask
for the things you really want?
Or will you get into trouble
just for asking?

What Christians want
more than anything else
is to know God better.

They also want to ask God
to give them the things
they need.
They want God to keep
them safe, to help them to
live in the right way
and to help other people.

They want God to take care of the world.
They want God's help
to tell other people about Jesus.
They know that God wants
to do all these things for them.

*Don't worry
about anything,
but pray to God
and ask him
for everything
you need,
and thank him
for his goodness.*

**From the letter Paul wrote to the first
Christians in the city of Philippi**

**Christians ask God for
the things they need —
on their own and
together as a church.**

9 Let's look at
Living as a family

In a loving family
people work together
and really help each other.

The Bible tells Christians to help each other
like members of a family.
Because each person is different,
everyone has a special gift to share,
and each one of them is important.

God has given
each Christian
a different job to do
in the church family.
For example,
some are able to teach others
more about God,
some are good at sharing
their things,
some know how to encourage
others,
some are good at welcoming
people into their homes.
God tells his family to
celebrate with people who
are happy
and to comfort those who are
sad.

**From the letter Paul wrote to the
first Christians in Rome**

**The family of Christians care
for one another and for other
people in everyday ways.**

Celebrating!

The best way
to celebrate good news
is to have a party!

The good news
that Christians share
is that God has given them
a new beginning in life.
They know they are children of God
and that they are with God
for ever.

Everyone is welcome
to join God's family.
It is a life full of joy
which makes them want to sing.
Christians love to celebrate together.

*Give thanks to God;
sing psalms, and hymns
and songs of praise.*

**From the letter Paul wrote to the
first Christians in the city of Colossae**

There are special celebrations at times like Christmas, when Christians remember Jesus' birth. At Easter, they are sad because Jesus was killed, and then they celebrate because God gave him new life.

Christians celebrate together, and sing joyful songs. They have festivals to remember special events.

11 Let's look at

Good news

If you have good news
you want to tell everyone.
You don't sit in a corner
wondering if people will ask
what you're thinking about.
You just have to tell them
out loud.

Christians have good news to tell:
that Jesus loves everyone
and that anyone who believes in him
can be really happy
because God accepts them into his family
and gives them a new start.
Jesus said this to the friends who first believed in
him:

*Go out to everyone
and tell them about me
so they can follow me.*

**From the book Matthew wrote
about Jesus**

**Christians want to tell
other people about
Jesus Christ.**

12 Let's look at

Words or actions?

It's one thing
to *say* you want to be good.
But it's when you show this
by doing good things
that people really believe you.

God wants everyone to be good
and to do good things:
God's family must be different
from those people who choose to
do wrong.
God wants them to be loving and
kind,
unselfish and fair,
to speak kindly,
to share what they have,
to help those in need.

In this way they can show people
a little of what God's love is like.
And they provide an example
of how God wants people to live.

Christians must live shining lives,
like stars lighting up the sky.

From the letter Paul wrote to the
first Christians in the city of Philippi

Christians want to please God by doing good
so everyone can see what he is like.

Grandparents

Your family
is not just you
and your parents,
but also your grandparents
and great-grandparents...
people from long ago, and far away.

The Christian family
includes everyone
who believes in Jesus:
from the first special friends he chose,
those who knew him as a man on this earth,
to people today who believe in him.

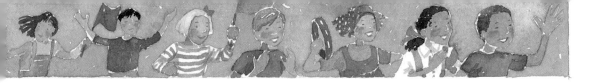

It includes all kinds of Christians
in countries all round the world
for 2,000 years.

Some are famous and remembered in
special stories,
others are not:
but they are all God's family
and God knows each one.
He has promised all of them
he will be with them for ever.

Nothing—
not even death—
can separate us
from the love of God.

From the letter Paul wrote to
Christians in Rome

The church is the family of Christians
throughout the ages.

What is the church?

1   **The church is the family of Christians.**

2   **When people join God's family, the church, they are making a new beginning.**

3   **Christians share bread and wine as a church, to remember Jesus — and that he gave his life for them.**

4   **Christians meet as a church to help and encourage each other.**

5   **Christians learn about God — on their own and together as a church.**

6   **Christians say sorry to God for the wrong things they have done — on their own and together as a church.**

7   **Christians say thank you to God for his goodness to them — on their own and together as a church.**

8   **Christians ask God for the things they need — on their own and together as a church.**

9   **The family of Christians care for one another and for other people in everyday ways.**

10   **Christians celebrate together, and sing joyful songs. They have festivals to remember special events.**

11   **Christians want to tell other people about Jesus Christ.**

12   **Christians want to please God by doing good so everyone can see what he is like.**

13   **The church is the family of Christians throughout the ages.**